MINI BOOK

A DOZEN A DAY

Technical Exercises
FOR THE PIANO
to be done each day
BEFORE *practicing*

by
Edna-Mae Burnam

THE WILLIS MUSIC COMPANY

P9-CQC-395

A DOZEN A DAY

The Dozen A Day Mini Book is planned to precede the Dozen A Day Preparatory Book.

In many years of teaching piano to the young student, I have found that there is a strong need for technical exercises right away, when they *begin* their piano lessons.

In the past I have been giving my beginning students technical exercises by rote until they were able to read the notes in a Dozen A Day Preparatory Book.

Now I feel there is a need for a Dozen A Day Mini Book to be used when they are beginners.

The Dozen A Day Mini Book is designed for use with any beginning method or series book one for either class or private instruction.

The exercises are built on the notes the student is learning to read so they will be able to read the notes in the Mini Book as they enjoy doing their Dozen A Day Mini exercises.

When a student has completed this book they will be ready to enjoy A Dozen A Day Preparatory Book.

EDNA-MAE BURNAM

A DOZEN A DAY

Many people do exercises every morning before they go to work.

Likewise - we should give our fingers exercises every day BEFORE we begin our practicing.

The purpose of this book is to help develop strong hands and flexible fingers.

Do not try to learn the entire first dozen exercises the first week you study this book! Just learn two or three exercises, and do them each day *before* practicing. When these are mastered, add another, then another, and keep adding until the twelve can be played perfectly.

When the first dozen - or Group I - has been mastered and perfected, Group II may be introduced in the same manner, and so on for the other Groups.

Many of these exercises may be transposed to different keys. In fact, this should be encouraged.

EDNA-MAE BURNAM

INDEX

PAGE

To my family

Group I
1. Walking

2. Hopping

3. Bouncing A Ball With Right Hand

© 2002 by The Willis Music Company
International Copyright Secured
Printed in the U.S.A.

4. Bouncing A Ball With Left Hand

5. Rolling

6. Arms Up And Down

7. Skipping

8. Deep Breathing

9. Hammering With Right Hand

Set thumb down silent.
Hold down throughout exercise.

10. Hammering With Left Hand

Set thumb down silent.
Hold down throughout exercise.

11. Walking In A Water Puddle In Boots

12. Fit As A Fiddle And Ready To Go

Group II
1. Twisting Right And Left

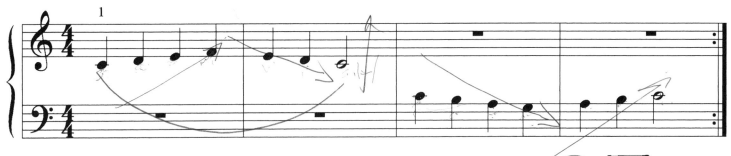

2. Flinging Arms Out And Back

3. Touching Toes

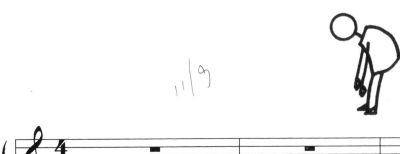

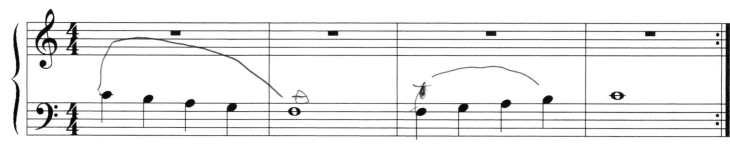

7. Stretching Legs Out And Back (sitting down)

8. Skipping

9. Deep Breathing

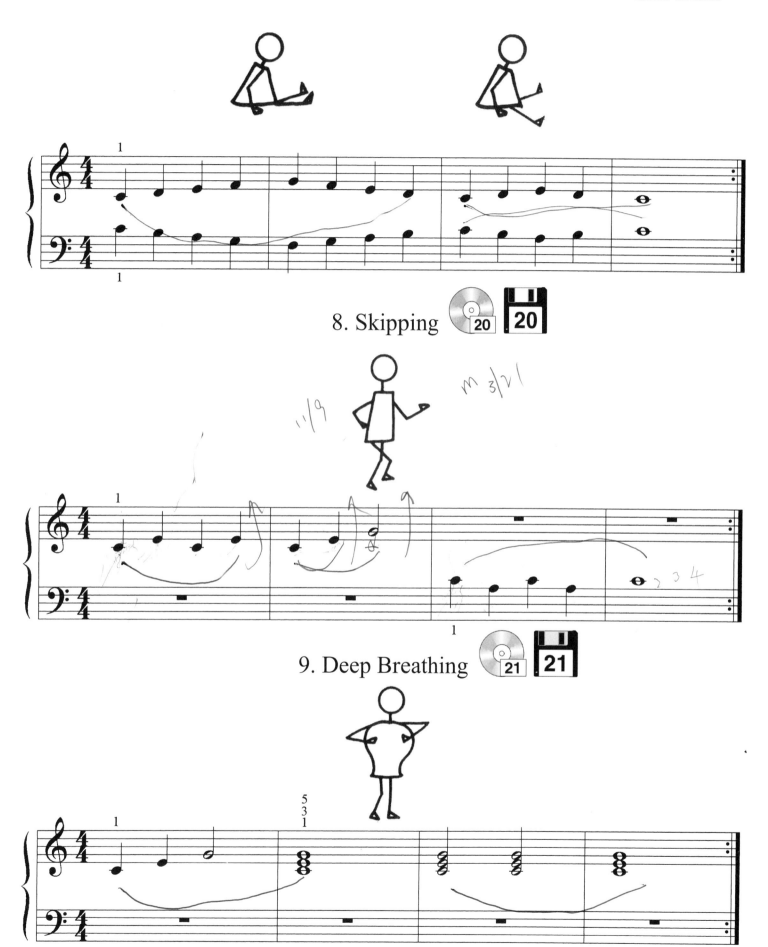

12

10. Jump Rope

11. Walking Down A Hill

12. Fit As A Fiddle And Ready To Go

Now I'm nim-ble as can be. I can play this mel - o - dy.

10015

Group III
1. The Splits

2. Deep Breathing

3. Wide Walk (Stiff Legged)

14

4. Right Knee Up And Back (Lying Down)

5. Left Knee Up And Back (Lying Down)

6. Both Knees Up And Back (Lying Down)

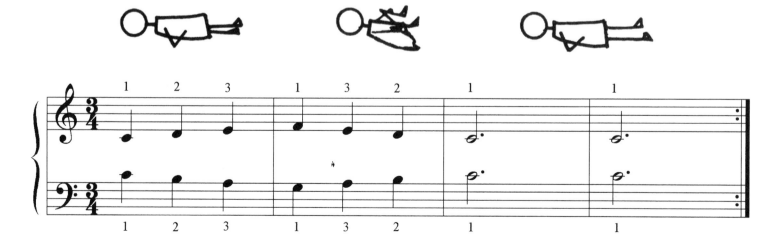

7. Backward Bend

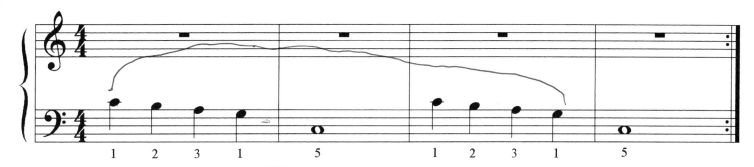

8. Twirling To The Right

9. Twirling To The Left

Group IV

1. Walking On A Sunny Day

2. Walking On A Cloudy Day

3. Skipping On A Sunny Day

18

10015

7. Baby Steps

8. Cartwheels

9. Leap Frog

10. Tight Rope Walking

Silent change.
Keep key down while
changing fingers.

11. Walking On Tip Toes

12. Fit As A Fiddle And Ready To Go

Fin - gers read - y   as   can   be.   Play - ing mus - ic   just   for   me.

4

Group V
1. Running

2. In A Swing

3. Teeter Totter

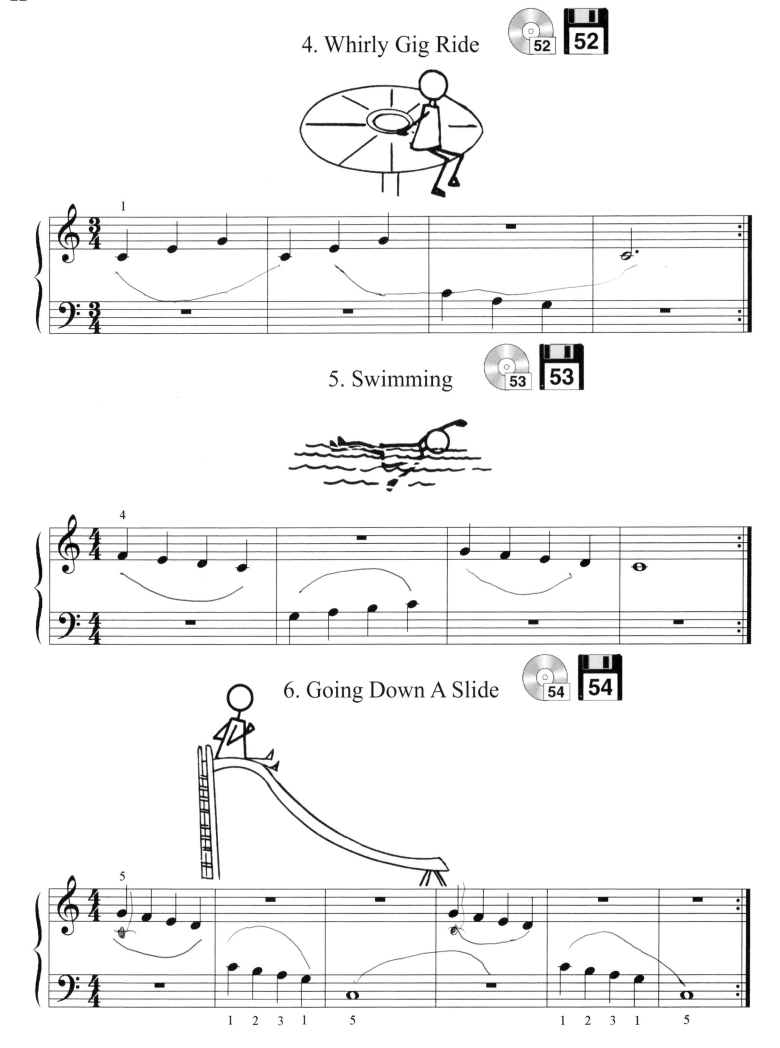

4. Whirly Gig Ride

5. Swimming

6. Going Down A Slide

23

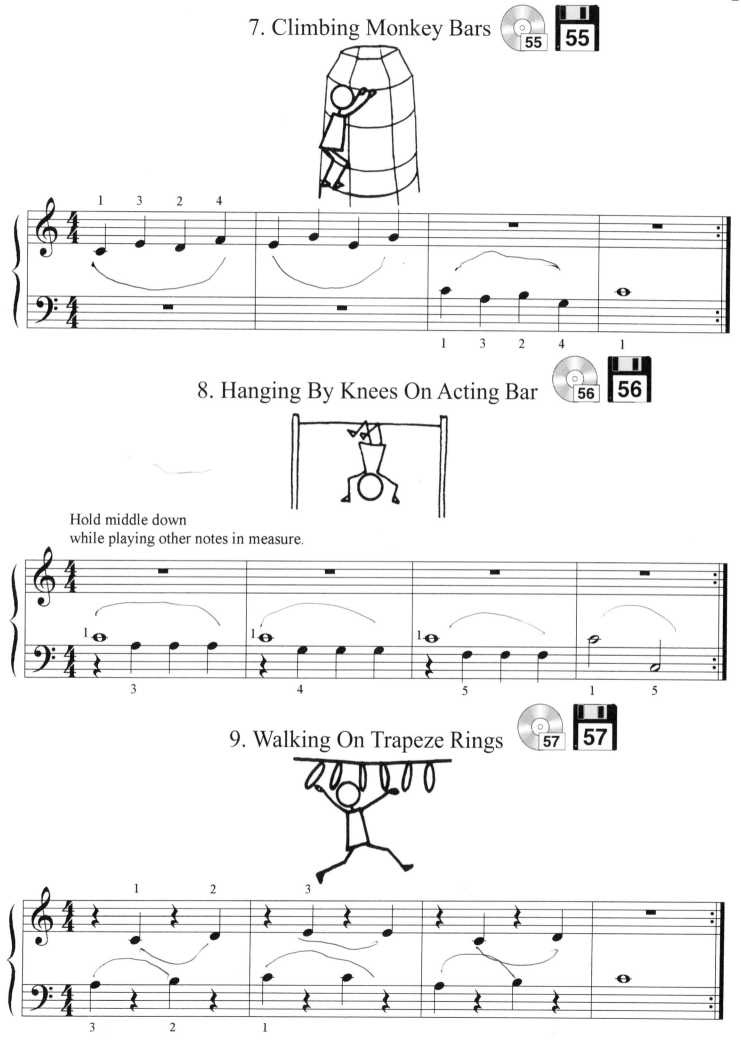

7. Climbing Monkey Bars

8. Hanging By Knees On Acting Bar

Hold middle down
while playing other notes in measure.

9. Walking On Trapeze Rings

0015

10. Jump Rope

11. Tether Ball

12. Fit As A Fiddle And Ready To Go

Nim - ble, nim - ble fin - gers like to play Lots of nim - ble notes to - day.